Ter
about Gardens

ex libris

Candlestick Press

Published by:
Candlestick Press,
Diversity House, 72 Nottingham Road, Arnold, Nottingham NG5 6LF
www.candlestickpress.co.uk

Design and typesetting by Craig Twigg

Printed by Ratcliff & Roper Print Group, Nottinghamshire, UK

Introduction: © Monty Don, 2011

Cover illustration © Rosalind Bliss, 2011
www.rosalindbliss.co.uk

Candlestick Press monogram © Barbara Shaw, 2008

© Candlestick Press, 2011

First Published 2011
Reprinted 2012 (twice), 2013, 2014, 2015, 2016, 2017, 2018, 2019,
2020

ISBN: 978 1 907598 07 4

Acknowledgements:

Candlestick Press wishes to thank Monty Don for his Introduction.
We raise a trowel in his honour.

Poems are reprinted by kind permission of Vikram Seth for 'The
Master-of-Nets Garden' from *The Humble Administrator's Garden*,
Carcanet Press, 1985; Louise Glück for 'Vespers' from *The Wild Iris*,
Carcanet Press, 1992; Ann Drysdale for 'New Fruit' from *Backwork*,
Peterloo Poets, 2002. 'Allotments' by Richard Church appeared in
Modern Poetry 1922 – 1934, Macmillan, 1934, and is reproduced
here by permission of Pollinger Limited. Our thanks also to Maura
Dooley and Bloodaxe Books for permission to reprint 'Sub Rosa' from
Sound Barrier, Poems 1982 – 2002, Bloodaxe Books, 2002. 'Ghost
of a Garden' © Robin Robertson, 2006, is reprinted from *Swithering*,
Picador, 2006 and 'Procrastination' is reproduced by kind permission of
Barbara Daniels (www.FormalPoetryetc.com) and Shoestring Press from
The Cartographer Sleeps, Shoestring Press, 2005.

Where poets are no longer living, their dates are given.

Contents

Introduction

Almost everything that is written about gardens and gardening is prosaic and practical. There is – and always has been – an obsession with horticultural technique and practice although whenever I meet wise and experienced gardeners, they invariably confess to knowing less and less the more that they garden.

But anyone who has ever loved a garden knows that this love cannot be properly expressed in prose. Words grope and struggle with meaning and it is the spaces between where the light falls best. Good gardening always aspires to poetry and horticultural technique should always be worn gossamer light. Good gardening - where goodness is measured by the capturing of the moment perfectly married between human nurture and untrammelled nature - needs poetry to capture, measure and catalogue it as surely as a list of seeds or plants.

That is what this little volume does perfectly. It is a garden catalogue and a manual spelling out the really important horticultural skills. And for those of us who garden to be fully human, to be sane, these are skills worth daily bending one's back to. The poetry comes as a gift 'like bright light through the bare tree' as in Louise Glück's 'Vespers' but is also acquired slowly as earthy prayer. The poetry is in the gardening as much as it is out in the garden, hinted at, barely caught, but understood completely.

These are all fine poems, all perfectly practical celebrations of why and how to garden. Read them with soil under your nails and to cultivate all that grows within. Read them and go out and garden the better for it.

Monty Don

Inscription for a Moss-House in the Shrubbery at Weston

Here, free from riot's hated noise,
Be mine, ye calmer, purer joys
    A book or friend bestows;
Far from the storms that shake the great,
Contentment's gale shall fan my seat,
    And sweeten my repose.

William Cowper (1731 – 1800)

Inscription for the Moss-Hut at Dove Cottage

No whimsy of the purse is here,
No pleasure-house forlorn;
Use, comfort, do this roof endear;
A tributary shed to cheer
The little cottage that is near,
To help it and adorn.

William Wordsworth (1770 – 1850)

The Master-of-Nets Garden

Magnolia petals fall, pale, fragrant, brown,
Resting on moss within a square of white;
Courtyard of quietness, of intimate stone
And latticed shadow. Outside, low at night,
Three moons – of water, mirror, sky – define
Pine and old cypress struggling against the stars,
And jasmine and gardenia combine
Their scent with that of closed magnolias.

Vikram Seth

New Fruit

In the last knockings of the evening sun
Eve drinks Calvados. Elsewhere in her life
She has played muse and mistress, bitch and wife.
Now all that gunpoint gamesmanship is done.
She loves the garden at this time of day.
Raising her third glass up to God, she grins;
If this is her come-uppance for her sins
It's worth a little angst along the way.
A fourth. Again the cork's slow squeaky kiss.
If, as the liquor tempts her to believe,
The Lord has one more Adam up His sleeve
He's going to have to take her as she is –
Out in the garden in a dressing-gown
Breathing old apples as the sun goes down.

Ann Drysdale

Of his Mistress, upon Occasion of her Walking in a Garden

My lady's presence makes the roses red,
Because to see her lips they blush for shame:
The lily's leaves, for envy, pale became,
And her white hands in them this envy bred.
The marigold abroad her leaves doth spread,
Because the sun's and her power is the same;
The violet of purple colour came,
Dyed with the blood she made my heart to shed.
In brief, all flowers from her their virtue take:
From her sweet breath their sweet smells do proceed.
The living heat which her eye-beams do make
Warmeth the ground, and quickeneth the seed.
The rain wherewith she watereth these flowers
Falls from mine eyes, which she dissolves in showers.

Henry Constable (1562 – 1613)

Allotments

Lifting through the broken clouds there shot
A searching beam of golden sunset-shine.
It swept the town allotments, plot by plot,
And all the digging clerks became divine –
Stood up like heroes with their spades of brass,
Turning the ore that made the realms of Spain!
So shone they for a moment. Then, alas!
The cloud-rift closed; and they were clerks again.

Richard Church (1893 – 1972)

To a Gardener

Friend, in my mountain-side demesne
My plain-beholding, rosy, green
And linnet-haunted garden-ground,
Let still the esculents abound.
Let first the onion flourish there,
Rose among roots, the maiden-fair,
Wine-scented and poetic soul
Of the capacious salad bowl.
Let thyme the mountaineer – to dress
The tinier birds – and wading cress,
The lover of the shallow brook,
From all my plots and borders look.

Nor crisp and ruddy radish, nor
Pease-cods for the child's pinafore
Be lacking; nor of salad clan
The last and least that ever ran
About great nature's garden-beds.
Nor thence be missed the speary heads
Of artichoke; nor thence the bean
That gathered innocent and green
Outsavours the belauded pea.

These tend, I prithee; and for me,
Thy most long-suffering master, bring
In April, when the linnets sing
And the days lengthen more and more
At sundown to the garden door.
And I, being provided thus,
Shall, with superb asparagus,
A book, a taper, and a cup
Of country wine, divinely sup.

Robert Louis Stevenson (1850 – 1894)

Sub Rosa

At Sissinghurst we are meant to gasp at
the borders. No-one could fail to notice the
bulging veins of clematis shinning up and over
so much powdery red brick. Who could be
unimpressed by the swags of roses, carpets of camomile,
the best Sunday manners of it all? But we came
with our vague idea of Vita, Virginia, a friendship
under trees. Little of that left here, between
the roped-off library books, a shop exhaling pot-pourri,
scones leaning patiently on loaded plates.

We let ourselves out by the back gate, follow
the Lakeside Walk till it collapses into nettles,
then fall down too, stretched out beneath
the cleanliness of trees, beside a scummy pool.
Water like pea soup, bright and green, on which
a single grebe is turning, leaving no wake.
Water where, weighed down with sorrows or stones,
the weed might part for you, close over your head silently.
Back in the garden the borders are busy with bees,
the air is humming with auto-rewinds, china and small change
chatter cosily, passion rots quietly under the rose.

Maura Dooley

Vespers

I don't wonder where you are anymore.
You're in the garden; you're where John is,
in the dirt, abstracted, holding his green trowel.
This is how he gardens: fifteen minutes of intense effort,
fifteen minutes of ecstatic contemplation. Sometimes
I work beside him, doing the shade chores,
weeding, thinning the lettuces; sometimes I watch
from the porch near the upper garden until twilight makes
lamps of the first lilies: all this time,
peace never leaves him. But it rushes through me,
not as sustenance the flower holds
but like bright light through the bare tree.

Louise Glück

Ghost of a Garden

Sometimes I discover I have gone downstairs,
crossed the grass and found myself
in here: the tool-shed,
caught in a lash of brambles, bindweed
and tall ivied trees like pipecleaners. It looks out,
vacantly, on a garden run to seed:
the lost tennis court, grown-over benches,
a sunken barbecue snagged with blown roses.
The courtyard walls are full of holes the swallows
try to sew, in and out of them like open doors.
In the corner of the shed my father is weeping
and I cannot help him because he is dead.

Robin Robertson

Procrastination

The old shed, in the corner, shadowed now
by sycamores and beech leaves, dark and cool,
waits for the sun to climb above that bough,
beam in through cobwebbed windows, warm the tools'
smoothed handles, ready for my hands. I wait
a little longer for the heavy heat,
leave spades alone until it is too late,
let spiders silk them over. Sacks of peat
spill open, compost dries; the smell of sheds
at noon is like a manacle. I'm trapped
by broken rakes, empty seed-trays. My head
buzzes with sleep-thoughts...musty...must...perhaps...
    I dream of camomile: no need to mow
    my cruel lawn today – or tomorrow.

Barbara Daniels

Out in the Garden

Out in the garden,
Out in the windy, swinging dark,
Under the trees and over the flower-beds,
Over the grass and under the hedge border,
Someone is sweeping, sweeping,
Some old gardener.
Out in the windy, swinging dark,
Someone is secretly putting in order,
Someone is creeping, creeping.

Katherine Mansfield (1888 – 1923)